BEYOND GOODBYE

BEYOND GOODBYE

Living
IN THE
Experience
of Loss

JEANNE BUNDY

gatekeeper press

Columbus, Ohio

BEYOND GOODBYE

Living in the Experience of Loss

Published by Gatekeeper Press

2167 Stringtown Rd, Suite 109

Columbus, OH 43123-2989

www.GatekeeperPress.com

Library of Congress Control Number: 2022937131

ISBN (paperback): 9781662927997

eISBN: 9781662928000

CONTENTS

PREFACE

Life can change in the blink of an eye.

People say this all the time, but it's hard to believe — hard to know what it really means — until you experience it for yourself. Until it becomes your reality.

When you lose someone you love, someone who is so much a part of you that their absence seems impossible, the lines between you and the rest of the world become blurred for a while. Life goes on around you. You see it. You acknowledge it. But starting to interact with it again... That's the hard part. Where do you even begin?

In 2019, after having lost two of the most important people in my life, that was one of many questions I found myself asking: Where do I begin? How do I start to heal myself enough to exist in this world that seems incredibly distant from what it was not so long ago? What is the first step toward moving not on or away, but through and forward?

I will you tell you up front that I am not a physician or a psychologist, nor do I have any formal training in mental healthcare. In answering these questions, I can only go by my journey. I can only share what I have felt and learned and embraced over the past few years. But if all you need is a starting point — a place from which to begin looking inward and engaging with your thoughts and emotions so that you can uncover your *own* answers — I hope you will find it within these pages. At the very least, I can guarantee that you will find a true story. My story.

The Beginning

I guess an introduction is as good a place to start as any, so let me tell you a bit about myself and two of the most important souls I have ever known.

My name is Jeanne — pronounced "Jeann-ie," though some people just call me "Jean." I grew up in Rhode Island, and I have a beautiful family full of extraordinary, caring, irreplaceable people. I've always considered myself fortunate.

In March of 2019, everything changed when the first of my two best friends died. My mom was my shopping companion, my lunch date, my advisor, my bosom buddy. She was 90 when it happened, but she was not your typical 90-year-old. She cooked. She baked. She crafted. She shopped. Her energy was unbelievable.

The illness came out of nowhere. She was sick for two days before her kidneys failed, and once at the hospital, she chose not to undergo dialysis, saying that she was just too tired. Within a week, she was gone. I didn't leave her side that entire time. I owed her too much. When you lose your mother or the mother figure in your life, it changes you in ways you can't express... But that is another book to write.

Eight months later, on December 15, my husband, William Francis Bundy — "Will," as I called him — had a massive heart attack and died in front of me, on our kitchen floor. Somehow, the fact that it happened in such a normal place made it all the more incomprehensible.

Will was a naval officer, and when he retired from the military, he became a professor at a prestigious college. I, on the other hand, made my way in a more personal field, as a hair stylist. He was pretty conservative; I've always been a free spirit. In other words, we were a great match!

My husband was my other best friend, my companion, my mentor, my *life*. I believe we were soulmates, each of us bringing the other a missing piece. We had two sons together. We traveled and lived all over the world together. By the time he passed, we had been married for over four decades. If my mother's death had been a shock, his was an absolute bombshell.

So, grief hit me with the force of a one-two punch that will be internally expressed forever. Within less than one year, I had lost the people who had been holding my world together in ways I didn't recognize until they were gone. How could I even imagine forming an existence without them when I was finding it hard to see straight, to speak, to breathe?

This is where my journey begins.

GRIEF AND NUMBNESS

Grief. It's such a tiny word, yet it has such a powerful meaning.

When people discuss how grief must be "processed," I wonder if they know what that means, or if they've ever actually felt it. I want to ask them if they've ever experienced a loss so deep that their heart broke into tiny pieces — pieces scattered so far apart that they wouldn't even know where to search for them, let alone where to find emotional glue strong enough to start putting them back together.

Grief is the direct result of loss. It is a state of being without something you once had; a stark realization that something is missing. Though I will only be speaking to the variety of grief that results from the death of a loved one, it can be caused by the loss of any dear thing — an animal, a home, a career, a physical ability, etc. It can be intense, it can be mild, or it can be somewhere in between. Mine was pretty intense.

I have come to understand grief as a living thing that we need not only to survive through, but to bloom beyond; something that we need to acknowledge and to fully feel so that we can thrust forward, onto the other side. Is this an overnight process? No, it is not. Moving through grief takes a while, and the amount of time is different for everyone. Some people move quickly. Some move slowly. Some never move at all.

Grief first hit me as numbness — or, as some might refer to it, shock. It's that "this shit is not real" feeling; total disbelief that a person who had so recently been a vibrant, vital, tangible part of your life could be gone; a fog that permeates your brain and stretches on indefinitely.

For me, the numbness lasted about a week or so. During that period, people seemed to understand that I basically had no mind with which to function. Meals were brought to my home, decisions were made for me, and I simply survived through it.

Sometimes, I wonder if numbness isn't such a bad place to be. It's a sort of natural bubble of protection, I think; a condition of existence (or of not actually existing) that allows you to deal with the bizarre making of arrangements and with the flood of sympathies coming from everyone you've ever known. You don't have to deal with your emotions yet because you can't remember what it's like to have them. You are just a body operating on the most basic level. Things are surreal. But they are simple.

This existential limbo, though — it is not a place where you are meant to stay for too long. Eventually, your system will begin to absorb the reality, bit by bit. And that's when the next phase hits you. That's when you learn about sadness.

SADNESS AND LAUGHTER

Looking back, I think the hardest part of grieving for me was leaving the snug cocoon of numbness for the hollow pit of sadness. It wasn't a conscious choice. It happened naturally, and once it did, I wanted to go back to not feeling. But I couldn't.

Sadness that cracks your heart in half, a sadness so overwhelming that you just do not know what to do with it — how do you overcome that? You don't. Sadness is an instinctive response to trauma. Whether a trauma is big or small, it hurts, and there will be a reaction to that pain.

In my case, that meant crying. I cried and cried and cried, for days and nights on end. When I thought there were no more tears, guess what? There they were, stored up like river water determined to break every dam in its path. At a certain point, I started to feel shame about this unshakeable habit, so I resorted to what I call "sneak crying": I played it cool and collected while I was in the company of others so that they wouldn't worry or feel bad, then I melted into a puddle of tears the second I was on my own again. This tactic worked for a time, but I knew that it wasn't sustainable. I couldn't keep swimming in my sadness. I knew that I would eventually need to find dry land again.

I should emphasize my belief that we never really forget sadness once we've experienced the deepest form of it. When we're in the throes of grief, sadness can seem like the only emotion available to us. It feeds on itself in such a way that it can almost become addictive, blinding and deafening us to alternative sensations. But we can learn to move beyond its overwhelming grip by allowing for the possibility of other feelings — and by gently kindling their sparks.

It's all about choice. At a certain point, I chose to set sadness aside, and I still make that choice every day. I know that it will always be there, and that I will grapple with it off and on for the rest of my life. I also now know that it will not consume me as long as I continue to choose other emotions over it.

The first moment of choice for me could have gone terribly wrong. A little over two months after my husband passed, you see, the COVID-19 pandemic took hold in the United States. The country quickly went into lockdown, and there I was alone in my house, with my grief and my cat and a treasure trove of once happy, suddenly heavy memories.

Like everyone else, I was allowed to go out only to purchase essentials. This meant something very different for me than for my neighbors, though. While other people were stockpiling toilet paper like it was gold, I was hunting down facial tissues. Of course, those soon became priceless, too, but in the early days of the crisis, I scored boxes and boxes of them.

So, that was my first choice: Kleenex or toilet paper? Kleenex won out. I mean, how else was I going to wipe away my endless tears and blow my runny nose?

My second choice was less obvious. My second choice was to laugh about my first one, even if only on the inside. Determining that crying was more of a concern for me than using the bathroom was such a basic reality check that I had to crack a smile. Maybe, I thought, my priorities were kind of... askew. Maybe it was time for me to feel like a human again — like someone who needed toilet paper as desperately as everybody else.

It was a scary thought, taking off the mantle of sadness and engaging with the fundamentals of life again, and if anyone had ever told me not to feel sad, I would not have been able to listen. I won't tell you not to feel sad, either. But I will tell you that seizing even the smallest opportunity for laughter makes it a little easier to realize that you can feel other things, too.

CHOICE

I want to circle back to something that I may have breezed by too easily in the last chapter: the idea of choice. We take it for granted, and given how many tiny decisions we make every day, that's not surprising. Pancakes or waffles? The blue shirt or the yellow one? Left turn, right turn? When life is cruising along as usual, we might be inclined to view the array of options available to us and the decisions we must make about them as blessings rather than burdens — if we chance to notice them at all.

When loss strikes, though, the seemingly simple ability to choose anything goes straight out the window. Our reality is not what it once was, so the normal rules don't apply. How can we address what to have for breakfast when we're suddenly faced with having it alone for the first time in...??? What *are* "blue" and "yellow"? And aren't left and right the same direction?

Immediately after a loss, the focus of our lives shifts back to basics. For me, that meant keeping my mind stable — and that was enough of a challenge. "Normal" was no longer a thing at that point, and the pandemic intensified that fact. My personal existence was not there anymore. There was a void.

That's what loss and grief are: a void; a black hole into which we are sucked with all the things that once defined our world. No quantity of pancakes can stop it up. No color will make it less gray. We can spend hours walking around in it without getting anywhere.

As physical beings, we will naturally seek out something tangible — a face or an arm or a voice that we can see, touch, or hear — to eliminate the void. But following a loss, those concrete things are no longer available to us, and the space in our hearts that they used to occupy so perfectly is just... empty.

That's where choice comes in. Choice is our lifeline — is *your* lifeline. You *can* climb out of the black hole. You *can* fill the void. But you have to make the choice to do so because no one else can make it for you. Yes, you will probably backslide every once in awhile. I certainly did, and I learned to accept it. Loss is an experience that we live through, not an isolated event with a definite beginning and end. It is a constant lesson. It calls for self-awareness, self-compassion, patience, and trust. All of those things are choices, too, and as such, life after loss has the potential to become much more intentional than it once was.

I'm lucky that it didn't take me long to learn one of the most crucial truths about grieving: namely, that I could — that I had to — decide how I wanted to feel each day. I discovered that I couldn't control which emotions got out of bed with me in the morning, but I *could* choose how to handle them. With practice, it became easier for me to wake up sad or anxious, sit with that feeling for a few compassionate minutes, then say to myself, *Jeanne, you're going to be okay today.* And whenever I made the choice to be okay, I was. Eventually, I was able to start choosing to be happy. Time allowed me the opportunity — the kind of time that someone who hasn't been in the trenches of a traumatic loss might not be able to grasp.

Moving forward, you will notice choice as a theme throughout my story. I hope that in reading about it and observing the role it has played in my healing process, you will become comfortable enough with the concept that integrating it back into your own life will not be a daunting prospect. The decisions that I have made are, obviously, different from what yours or anyone else's will be. But the theory is the same: The more active you are in crafting your post-loss life, choice by choice, the more likely you are to begin to feel grounded within it.

IDENTITY

Once I had rediscovered my ability to choose, I had to wrap my mind around what to do with it. I was beginning to see that the choices we make every day, no matter how small they seem, are kind of a big deal. They determine — or reveal — who we are, which is something that becomes a giant question mark when we are looking loss head on.

With my husband having passed only eight months after my mother, I felt that I had lost more than just their physical presence; I had lost nearly my entire identity, too. I didn't realize how wholly I saw myself through the lens of my relationship to each of them until they were no longer around to reflect a picture back at me. I was a daughter, a wife, a best friend, the family cook, the resident party planner... and then I wasn't. I held so many job titles for so many years, and then they were just gone. Maybe other people still saw me as all those things, but I no longer felt that the labels belonged to me. Things had shifted on a fundamental level. I don't remember ever having been so internally off balance.

In retrospect, I view the situation as a bizarre, almost impossible puzzle, wherein the pieces seemed the same but didn't fit together the way they once had. I was still there. My environment was the same as it had always been. But the things that had once connected me to that environment and to my world as a whole no longer held any meaning.

Food shopping is a great example of this phenomenon because it's something everyone does without putting deep philosophical thought into it. When my husband was around, I filled my grocery cart with foods that he enjoyed. Some of them I learned to eat though I now realize that I never really liked them. Other items, like meat, posed more of a challenge. I don't eat meat, but I bought plenty of it for him — and then I ended up cooking two meals every night so that neither of us would starve.

The first time I trekked to the grocery store after Will's death was an enlightening experience. From the moment I walked through the door, I was on autopilot, unconsciously hunting down the foods I had always purchased. Then, somewhere between the deli and the bread aisle, it hit me like a smack in the face: Those were not my choices. There was no need to buy those things.

That was a startling revelation because it showed me just how fully I defined myself by the decisions I made based on what other people liked. In fact, they weren't decisions at all. I was just following orders — orders disguised as loving requests and hidden behind my desire to satisfy everyone. So... What the heck did I like? I had no clue. That information was buried under decades of not actually choosing anything at all. Funny, right?

Funny and scary. That was a turning point for me. It marked the start of my journey toward discovering who I really was — who I wanted to be. The notion that I could make decisions based on what *I* enjoyed was overwhelming at first. I was the only one I had to choose for, which was pretty heavy stuff considering that I had been operating like a pre-programmed machine for years, when there were other needs and opinions to take into account. Suddenly, I was on my own.

Think for a minute about how you would have described yourself before grief sucked your world away. Would you have painted a self-portrait from some external perspective, as I did? Would you have called yourself a parent, a sister, a spouse, a coworker, etc.? Do you still do this today, even after your loss?

Labels are not a bad thing in and of themselves. They help us to understand and organize our world. But it's important to question them because, convenient though they may be, they do not define us. They are not our identity. It is shocking to recognize how completely our self-image can become intertwined with that of other people and things — but once we do, we can begin the process of figuring out who we are beyond our relationships. We can begin to design our own reality.

OLD AND NEW

———————

So, this reality building business... I made up my mind to get brave and dive straight in; to determine who I was, what I wanted, and where I fit in the world now that I had started to strip away a lifetime of labels. Somehow, I knew that this needed to be my next step, and it was a big one. I had to get organized.

Writing lists of things I thought I liked and the reasons I thought I liked them became a constant exercise. Since I love to cook and eat, it made sense to begin with food because the choices were obvious. Back at the grocery store, in the frozen desserts aisle, for instance: Why, I asked myself, was I reaching for vanilla? I'm a chocolate gal. You get the idea.

After I conquered the refrigerator and pantry, I thought it was time to take a close look at each room of my home. The difficulty level here was higher than with food. At times, I found myself wanting to change everything, then ended up acknowledging that some things were the way they were for practical reasons. Spotting the line between personal preference and pragmatism was confusing, to say the least. But with practice, I got better at it.

My first official liberation came in the form of two bath towels and a bathroom rug. I think I always would have liked a different color scheme for the bathroom, but in a male-dominated household, the options seemed limited. So one day, I gave myself permission to choose — and I chose pink. More significantly, I chose to make myself (and the little girl inside me who really, really loves pink) feel good. To this day, walking into the bathroom and seeing it all done up in one of my favorite colors is incredibly satisfying.

Eventually, interior design became a game of addition and subtraction for me — keeping what worked, ditching what didn't, weaving in my tastes wherever possible. For now, I'm comfortable with the way it has all shaped up. When I no longer am, I will have the freedom to make a change. This is my new reality. It is a living, breathing thing, and it is constantly teaching me about myself.

In a way, this part of the healing experience has been like unraveling an extended memory that was coiled up in a dark, dusty corner of my mind. I had forgotten that chocolate did it for me in a way that vanilla, though perfectly pleasant, never could. I had left the little girl who adored pink behind sometime between my marriage and the arrival of my own children. I had allowed my personal likes and dislikes to become mere shadows, and the idea that I might be capable of cultivating new preferences hadn't even entered my head. But once I located that unremembered me, letting her out to explore was inevitable.

Now it's your turn, and you can begin by simply observing your habits and routines. Which ones actually belong to you and which ones belong or belonged to someone else? What have you forgotten? What have you been hiding behind the layers of labels attached to the relationships you've lost? *Who are you?* This is your time to remember, your time to explore and expand your world — your opportunity to take all the puzzle pieces that were scattered around you by grief and put them back together in a way that makes you feel happy and whole. It might even be an opportunity to build a new puzzle altogether.

I won't lie: The process will probably be neither quick nor painless, and I can't tell you how long it will go on. But if you start small, like I did, you can build up the confidence and the motivation to keep at it. In making your choices, be as subtle or bold as you feel you can be. I don't recommend changing too many things at once because you might end up exhausting yourself. If a pink bath towel catches your eye, though... Well, don't be afraid to buy it. Get comfortable with deciding for yourself, and know that it's okay to change your mind later. This is *your* life, after all. This is the new you.

FEAR

I've used the word "scary" in passing a couple of times so far, refer-ring both to the decision to start experiencing emotions again and to the deci-sion to start making decisions. We should take a closer look at this fear thing, though, because it's no joke.

Fear seems kind of ironic in the wake of a major loss. I mean, depending on how central the departed person was to our lives, we've probably already ex-perienced our greatest possible fear in the loss itself, right?

Not so much in my case. The notion that my two most bosom buddies might vanish within the space of a few months had just never occurred to me. First of all, I've never been a worrier. Second... Who would've thought? Yes, my mother had been getting on in years, but she was still such an active, vital force that I hadn't mentally prepared for her to check out when she did. And as for Will, there was just no lead-up; no obvious final chapter to the story of his life. It ended on a cliffhanger, and for a long time, I kept waiting for some sort of external resolution. (Spoiler alert: It never came — or not in the shape that I thought it would, anyway. More on that later.)

Of all the emotions that bubbled up for me as I braved this unexpected double whammy of grief, fear was the one that most caught me by surprise because, as I said, worrying had never been my thing. But I soon learned that fear feeds on sadness and shock. I also learned that it can present itself in many forms, and that we won't always recognize it when it does.

For me, it crept up so stealthily that I only ended up noticing it out of sheer boredom. Granted, a great deal of my grieving took place during the pandemic, when boredom was becoming a popular affliction. But it was not *my* MO. So one day, after rearranging the living room couch pillows for the fifth time, it struck me that even in the face of a global health crisis, I would have been doing things very differently had Will or my mom still been around. We would have been dreaming up ways to amuse ourselves — together. And just being in each other's company would have been a satisfying sort of diversion.

As it was, I found myself turning into that person who was uncertain if she could actually do things alone. I started to have anxiety about going places. I began to make excuses not to take a walk or go shopping or have dinner with family. Even opening my front door seemed like a risky proposition. I was, I realized, stopping myself from embarking on the simple, everyday adventures I used to enjoy.

Worse than that, this newfound fear had begun to fuel itself on a fundamental level, making me feel less like myself than I already did and prompting me to question abilities that I had always regarded as pretty basic. Could I balance my checkbook? Of course I could. But some insidious post-loss voice told me that I couldn't. Did I know when to schedule an oil change — and was I capable of driving the car to the shop to get it done? Um, yes! But my bereft brain made me doubt my judgement.

When we are grieving, it is common for our fears to multiply, and once they do, it is easy for us to start to take them for the truth. I suspect that this readiness to distrust ourselves stems from the identity issue — from that natural tendency to define ourselves by the people and things around us, and to unknowingly rely on them for structure and safety. Don't get me wrong: Healthy relationships and a supportive network of family and friends are wonderful, even essential, things. Yet it is just as important for us to be aware of and have faith in our own strength; to believe, beyond the shadow of a doubt, that we can stand on our own two feet.

And so I ask you this: How is fear showing up in your life after loss? Where has it begun to seep through the cracks of your consciousness? Have you been avoiding activities that once gave you pleasure or postponing tasks that you used to accomplish without difficulty? And have you been telling yourself that you just don't feel like doing those things right now instead of acknowledging that you're *afraid* to do those things right now?

I encourage you to take the risk of facing your fears. Make time to sit with them and to recognize them for what they are. Then trust in your strength to work your way through them. I'm no superhero, so if I did it, you can, too — and I'll give you some ideas on how to go about it.

COURAGE

To some extent, conquering the grocery store fortified me. I came to view it as a little victory and a sort of training ground for my reentry into the realm of choice making. But once I settled into that routine, I knew I had much more to do — and that doing any of it would take courage.

So, I ventured to the local big box store, just to test my limits. I didn't even have to leave the driver's seat to run into them. The lot was gigantic. How was I going to remember where I had parked? What if I totally lost my car? What if I came out of the store with a cart full of booty and I had nowhere to put it?

Now, when I calmed down and thought about it, I had to acknowledge that my memory for such things had never been great. Knowing where I put so-and-so simply isn't a forte of mine. I have the same issue with driving directions. I can get lost with my GPS leading the way!

Trouble was that I hadn't had occasion to notice these shortcomings in ages because, up until that moment, I had made most of my excursions in the company of my husband. Will was incapable of forgetting where he had parked the car, and he could probably have driven from coast to coast without a map. But he wasn't around anymore. I had to figure it out.

Jeanne, I counseled myself as I sat staring through my windshield at the entrance to the store, *you can do this.* I took a deep breath, got out of the car, and looked closely at my surroundings, making note of things that would not be moving while I was in the store. A lamp post, a shopping cart corral, a line of trees on the other side of the lot — I took it all down with my mental pen. Then, for added assurance, I snapped a picture of my parked car with my phone.

To be honest, I can't remember if I had any trouble locating my car when I finished shopping that day because so many other anxieties were running through my mind as I braved the endless aisles and fluorescent exposure of the store. But from that point on, I made it a rule to follow the procedure of note making and picture taking whenever I had to park in an unfamiliar or crowded place. It would be my way of ensuring my safety and mental comfort when I was on my own.

I used a similar tactic in confronting my... oh, let's call them "directional challenges."

My husband passed away ten days before Christmas in 2019, so the whole family was still together, wading through the earliest stages of grief as a group, when the holiday arrived. That meant that I didn't truly feel Christmas loneliness until the following year, after about ten months of social distancing and periodic pandemic-related lockdowns. Not so suddenly, I found myself face to face with the prospect of an actual trip on my own: the hour-long drive to my son's house for lunch. "Terrified" doesn't begin to describe the sensation that swirled inside me when I tried to envision myself behind the wheel, navigating such a journey without my trusty copilot. *Nope*, my stomach told me. *Not happening.*

In this case, I'm glad I didn't listen to my gut. In its unsettled state, it would undoubtedly have kept me in my house, at my empty kitchen table, with my confused cat (who, like me, was still occasionally skeptical of the fact that there was only one human around to look after). Thinking about that day now, I am proud of the choice I made to overcome my fear — to bundle myself up in my favorite winter gear, buckle myself into the driver's seat, and hit the road.

Did I get lost? Yes. Twice. But the neat thing about GPS is that it barely misses a beat in rerouting you when you stray from the recommended course. So I made it to that Christmas lunch, and then I made it home again. Will would have been proud of me, too.

We have the opportunity to choose courage every day. That may sound daunting, but it doesn't have to be. Seek out tiny chances for brave choice making and start there — then be sure to congratulate yourself on your little wins.

If you shared financial responsibilities with the person you lost, for instance, maybe you're seriously struggling with the idea of staying on budget. Instead of letting fear stop you in your tracks, get practical about it, like I did. Determine what you need to do to remove the anxiety from the situation, or at least to lessen it, then take action. Do you have a friend or family member who can give you some guidance on personal bookkeeping? Is there an affordable online course you can take? The answer to both of those questions is probably "yes."

As another example, maybe your back yard is staring you down because the person who used to be in charge of the physically demanding labor — mowing, weed whacking, tree trimming, etc. — is no longer around. The great news is that lawn maintenance services are a dime a dozen, and chances are good that one of your neighbors can give you a solid recommendation. Or if you're in need of a wallet-friendly alternative, you can probably find an enterprising teenager in the area who's looking to make a few bucks after school. Both solutions require nothing more of you than the courage to set your pride and your fear of change aside so that you can ask for assistance.

Just as most of us have fears that we didn't know existed prior to our losses, we also all have resources — both external and internal — about which we may never have been aware. Be willing to call on and cultivate those resources so that you can begin to feel more confident in your own skin. Before you know it, you'll be ready to tackle bigger hurdles. You'll be ready for adventure.

ADVENTURE

As I continued to scale the mountain of my grief, making seemingly infinite discoveries about myself along the way, I began to realize that there was much more I wanted to accomplish in life — more than just figuring out how not to lose my car and how to survive a solo drive (with technological assistance, mind you).

So I grabbed my pen and set to list making again, jotting down all the things I wanted to do on one side of the page and my reasons for not having done them so far on the other. Some of the items were super simple — and most of my excuses for avoiding them looked pretty flimsy on paper. In general, they boiled down to that pesky, omnipresent feeling of fear: fear that I wouldn't understand how to do a particular thing, fear that I would make a mistake in attempting it, fear that I'd need to ask for help or have someone complete a task for me.

Hovering over it all was that reliable old fear of making choices. Not only did I have a whole host of to-dos to choose from; I also had to make the choice to actually *do* them. I had to stop tip-toeing around reality and find creative ways to ease back into it.

One of the most commonplace activities on my list was walking into a restaurant and eating by myself. I'm sure single people do this all the time, but I hadn't been single in over four decades! I needed a strategy.

First, I selected a situation that felt comfortable: a small outdoor art festival in my town. This, I reasoned, would give me a justification for being out and about, so if I lost my nerve... I pushed that "if" away. I'd have to get nervous about my nerves later.

When I arrived, I scoped out my surroundings and spotted a little, unintimidating café. *That should do it*, I thought. *Now or never, Jeanne.* I put on my game face and walked in. My hands were shaking. A ball of anxiety was sitting in my chest. But I did it. I ordered a muffin and a coffee, I sat down at a bistro table, and I enjoyed myself.

Was this, on the surface, a tiny choice? Sure. For me, though, it had a huge impact. It gave me the confidence to take a crack at other, more daunting items on my list. It made me feel more secure with the idea of experimenting. It was my ticket to adventure — even if my variety of adventure just looked like normal life to everyone else.

Obviously, I'm a fan of lists. But that's not just because I'm a natural organizer. It's because they can be highly effective in baby-stepping through the anxieties and doubts that so often accompany a major loss.

With that in mind, I ask you: What's on your life to-do list? If you don't have one yet, or if it only exists in your head, I suggest writing it down on paper, including your reasons for not attempting the items on it. The simple act of making your list tangible can help you to wrap your mind around tackling it, bit by bit, without self-judgement. Each time you accomplish a task, notice how it makes you feel — how it boosts your faith in your ability to do this whole living thing, with or without another person by your side.

As to what kind of items you put on your list, anything goes. If you've always wanted to see Fiji, but you haven't taken a vacation since your loss because the thought of going it alone petrifies you, just Google "groups for people who don't want to travel alone." Seriously. You'll find all kinds of options to explore, and you might even wind up making a few like-minded friends.

If there's a specific skill that you've long had an itch to pick up — a language or carpentry or how to make your own puff pastry, pasta, and pie crusts so that you can host fancy family dinners — now could be the ideal time to do so. Again, if the only barrier before you is the sheer terror of attempting the unknown on your own, hit the internet and find a class. I would be shocked if there isn't a course covering your exact interest.

Whatever is on your list and however you choose to approach it, don't let fear hold you back. Be bold. Be tenacious. Be yourself. Let your newfound courage take the lead so that you can venture forth freely.

SECURITY

Funny thing about all my adventuring and experimenting and testing of personally uncharted waters: Though I was gaining confidence in my competence as captain of my own life and in my capacity for creating a functional, fulfilling solo existence, my anxiety didn't disappear. It simply shifted to other areas of my consciousness — and at times, it seemed to have increased.

The more I waded through my complex web of emotions and the more I opened my mind to what was essentially a reinvention of self, the more the feeling of security became important to me. When thrown off balance, the human mind has a tendency to amplify or dramatize every little thing, and at some point, I started to feel physically unsafe on account of my internal upheaval.

My worry-driven, question-laden mental narrative ran the gamut from *Did I lock the door?* and *Are the windows* — all *of the windows* — *shut?* to *Can I make it to the mailbox and back without risk of mortal peril?* and *What happens if I forget my keys and can't get back into the house?* It got so bad that I could inevitably be found in my PJs with my entire home locked down like Fort Knox by sundown — even in the winter, when twilight fell around 4pm. I never went out after dark, and I made a point to close as many curtains as possible so that I wouldn't have to imagine what dangers might be lurking in my yard.

At first, I didn't notice what was going on. I just allowed the endless, swirling sea of anxiety to sweep me along because, to be honest, it all felt so natural. Why *shouldn't* I be concerned about my safety? I was, after all, a single woman living on my own. (Sorry, cat, but you don't count when it comes to ensuring personal protection.) My house was big and empty, and darkness just seemed so... dark.

But one night, as I was checking every external door lock for the third time, it dawned on me that circumstances were really not so different at that moment from what they had been when my husband was alive. The house was the same size. The sky outside was no more inky or opaque. The only true contrast was Will's absence.

Slowly, I acknowledged what I was doing and how irrational my behavior had become. I decided that this was just another manifestation of fear for me to face — another opportunity to make choices that would help me to heal rather than keep me literally locked in place. So, in accordance with my recently established fear-crushing strategy, I started small, allowing myself to bolt the doors at 4pm, but holding off on the PJ wardrobe change until 8pm. Then I coaxed myself into looking through a window or two once darkness had fallen so that I could get used to the view and to the idea that, though I couldn't see every little thing, there were probably no monsters out there.

Gradually, calling these shots began to make me feel more secure internally, and my tiny choices became bigger. As a prelude to the possibility that I might someday leave the house at night, I gave a spare key to a relative who lived in town so that if I ever found myself keyless on the wrong side of the door after normal locksmith hours, I had a solution. Eventually, I stopped locking up at 4pm. And in time, I made it to an evening dinner date at the home of a friend.

Learning to feel safe following a loss is an important step toward healing. It's crucial, however, to make the distinction between emotional safety and physical safety. Grief and pain and sorrow and fear can become pretty heavy security blankets if we surrender to them, and they can prevent us from admitting that we might be able to — that we might *want* to — experience pleasure and love and joy again.

My construction of a physical fortress was, in effect, an attempt to protect myself from the complicated feelings associated with reinventing my life minus two of the people who had long served as the glue holding it together. But as I began to let those external safeguards go, I found that it wasn't so bad to feel the things that I had once felt for and with my husband and mother again — things that I had subconsciously assumed could only exist in their presence. And better yet, I saw that allowing those emotions to flow freely did nothing to lessen the value of my relationships with those irreplaceable people. To this day, the memories we created together are still tucked away in my internal treasure chest, and they are still beautiful. I have simply made room for more of them.

Now over to you: Following your loss, when was the last time you ran a security check on your life? Have you put up any logistical barricades around yourself so that you don't have to confront uncomfortable or downright frightening obstacles within? If your answer is "yes," what small changes and choices can you make to begin breaking down unnecessary external barriers so that you can ultimately release the emotional ones, as well?

Maybe you feel unsafe in your own home, like I did. Well, what if you could have a sensible security system installed by a professional? What if you were to adopt a big dog with a bigger bark? What if you were to make friends with your next-door neighbors so that you could feel okay about calling them in the case of a real emergency?

Take the time to think about what will make you feel physically secure enough to put aside your external worries and any inhibiting habits you've built up around them before they spiral out of control. In doing so, you will allow yourself the space, the energy, and the strength to face the prospect of enjoying life again.

ANGER AND RESENTMENT

Speaking of finding joy again, there are a few tricky, intertwined emotions beyond fear and doubt that will inevitably delay our progress on that front. Two of the most potent are anger and resentment, and they often come as a convenient, complementary set. It can, in fact, be tough to figure out where one ends and the other begins.

The timing is different for everyone, but once we make it through the initial shock of a loss, anger and resentment are not far behind. We become so bent out of shape at the fact that such an injustice could occur that we start blaming our higher power, the world as a whole, inanimate objects... Anything that pops into our mind or our direct line of sight is fair game for our white-hot, unrelenting animosity.

Before loss and grief entered my life, I had rarely experienced anger, especially not the prolonged variety. I had never thought about it before then, but I guess it just wasn't in my genetic makeup to be mad. And as for resentment — well, that feeling was almost entirely foreign to me. Perhaps, like anger, bitterness simply wasn't in my blood. Or maybe I hadn't had any significant opportunities to hold a grudge in the six decades I had seen so far. Whatever the case, I was blindsided by the powerful punch these two sensations can pack.

As with many of my other grief-related emotions, I didn't realize that I was angry until the day my printer stopped working — or, as my mind chose to perceive it at the time, the day my printer positively *refused* to perform its duty when I urgently needed a hardcopy of a document. Having no idea how to fix the problem, I just sat alone, getting angrier and angrier at the printer for being so insubordinate, at myself for not being able to make it do my bidding, at fate for having taken my husband from me, at my husband himself for not being around to help me. At some point, I actually started yelling at Will for having died before showing me how to properly operate this blasted piece of office equipment.

And that's when it hit me: The absurdity of my outrage. How in the world was Will supposed to have foreseen this scenario? Did I really expect him, an aging but otherwise healthy, happy man, to have anticipated the heart attack that would prevent him from serving as my knight in jeans and flannel at this time of great need?

Not to minimize anyone's feelings — even my own — with regards to trauma, but as I look back on that moment, I have to laugh. I wanted to be rescued from the technology that I had never previously needed to understand on account of the amateur Mr. Fix-It who had long shared a roof with me. I was assuming that I was helpless without having entertained the possibility that I might be able to help myself. I was choosing to play the victim rather than the hero, and then I was getting steamed about it.

Once I made that realization, the flames of fury started to melt away, and I was able to see what I needed to do. I needed to change my choice — to grab my cape and come to my own rescue. So I turned to the good old internet, did a search on "how to fix a printer," and there it was: a step-by-step solution that I could actually comprehend. In less time than it had taken me to get worked up, I stood triumphant with that important document in my hand. I had resolved my crisis and pocketed a new skill in the process.

Now I'd like to rewind for a minute and draw attention to where the resentment fits into that story because, as I mentioned, it can be difficult to distinguish from anger. At the height of my rage, I began assigning blame — to the printer, to my husband, and to the fickle hands of fate. We can set the poor printer aside since it could have been anything, really; any item that happened to be in the immediate vicinity and that was not behaving as my unsteady mind thought that it should. But as for my husband and whatever intangible force might have been behind his untimely end...

When we lose a loved one, it is not at all uncommon to feel abandoned both by that person and by the invisible, omnipotent hand that removed them from our lives. Placing blame can provide a small amount of satisfaction and even comfort to a head and heart heavy with grief. Ultimately, however, blame is just a temporary, false balm for our emotional wounds, and the more we apply it, the more resentful we become.

My husband did not choose to have a heart attack, so accusing him of leaving me high and dry was neither accurate nor fair. And I could rail away at fate or some higher power for any number of injustices until I was blue in the face, but where would that leave me? I was born and raised Catholic, and though I no longer practice any specific religion, I have always maintained a strong belief that someone or something out in the universe has my back. I still look to the Divine for solace and guidance in trying times, and seeing as my version of the Divine would never intend to harm me and has yet to fail me, giving up on my faith out of resentment over some silly printer incident seemed a bit unreasonable. Okay, *really* unreasonable.

Keeping anger and resentment pent up is not healthy for anyone in any situation, but particularly not for someone in the midst of grief. In order to heal, we have to learn to release such sticky feelings so that they will, in turn, release us. For some people, this could entail screaming out loud or even throwing (non-breakable) objects at the floor. Others may find that writing it all down — holding nothing back and suspending self-judgement — helps to stem the infinite spiral of negativity. (Just remember: If your method of emotional release involves screaming, close your windows!)

Before you can think about letting anger and resentment go, though, it's important to understand where those feelings are coming from and what is really causing them. Are you angry at your partner, child, parent, etc. for having left you, like I was? Are you riled about the loss of reality as you once knew it? Are you just fuming at the world as a whole for continuing to turn indifferently while you deal with the fallout from your personal disaster?

Once you've identified the roots of these toxic emotions, you'll be able to start digging them up and discarding them. I'm not saying that they won't come back on occasion. Trust me: They will. But by learning to address them now, you will be making it easier for yourself to do so again in the future. Do you want to be in a temper all the time? Do you want to spend your energy holding grudges or assigning blame? Probably not. You can choose a different path. You can choose, as I did, to be your own hero — to rescue yourself from anger and resentment.

JEALOUSY AND GRATITUDE

As it turns out, there are many dimensions to resentment. Again, since I hadn't been personally exposed to the sensation prior to my losses, this was more news to me.

Resentment's ugly stepsister, jealousy, came at me out of nowhere, just as anger had. Or so I thought. Like every other emotion I encountered on the rollercoaster of grief, I imagine that this one was building up within me for a while before it reached its peak and sent me plummeting into a mire of outwardly directed negativity.

It didn't really hit me until I was scrolling through social media after a holiday. Even with the pandemic still looming over the globe, people were trying to get together in whatever ways they could, and I found myself looking in on friends enjoying the company of each other and their families, on kids being shown off by loving parents, on doting grandparents meeting grandchildren for the first time. There were also people happily reporting on huge promotions, major relocations, or skills developed during lockdown and converted into new careers.

In an earlier era, I probably would have felt nothing but joy in witnessing such beautiful events and journeys unfolding before me. My initial grief-stained reaction, however, was on the other end of the spectrum. I could identify a deep sadness in the pit of my stomach, but there was something else, too. I remember narrowing my eyes at each photo and thinking, *Yes, you're happy now, but just you wait. Everything can change in an instant.* It was as though I needed to knock these fortunate souls, many of them dear friends, down a peg; to make them understand that all good things must end, and that relationships and love and happiness are only as permanent as the people who experience them — which is to say not permanent in any way.

As you might imagine, this was not a pleasant sensation. And yet I kept right on scrolling, digging myself deeper and deeper into a bottomless pit of... What was it that I was actually feeling? Having already endured my fair share of discomfort in recent months, I knew that I couldn't just push the emotion down and walk away because it would inevitably haunt me until I confronted it. So I chose to pull it apart, strand by strand, seeking its serpentine roots.

I felt sad. That was easy enough to determine. I also felt amazed that other people could be going about the business of living so lightheartedly, as though death didn't exist — as though my losses hadn't happened. And beyond that amazement, there was annoyance at their ignorance and insensitivity and the very fact that they "had" where I "had not." But what was that annoyance, really?

Aha, I thought with reluctant satisfaction. *There it is: resentment.*

This resentment, however, had a different slant to it than that which I had felt toward my husband during the printer incident. In this case, I realized, I was *jealous* of the happy couples and the proud grandparents and even the giggling babies; of the recent home purchases and the job promotions and the creative accomplishments. This startled me.

Jealousy, Jeanne? Really? Hold up. You've been there. You've done that. Where is all this envy coming from? It doesn't even make sense!

And it truly didn't. I reminded myself that I had already gone through the baby thing (twice), that my affection and gratitude for my children would never fade, and that no amount of money or chocolate could persuade me to stay up with a screaming infant or fight over bedtimes or wage wars over unfinished homework ever again. I had also enjoyed a successful and rewarding career, had traveled and lived all over the world, had seen and done and learned many wonderful things with the people I loved most. In other words, I was missing what I already had. I was trying to fill the internal space left by my losses with my emotional responses to experiences and memories that didn't belong to me, forgetting that I had an ample supply of my own.

At that point, I decided to dig out some old photo albums and take a little trip into my personal history. As I flipped through dozens upon dozens of pictures, through countless blissful moments frozen in time, tears poured down my face. I felt such gratitude for the privilege of my relationships — for having married my soulmate and savored forty marvelous years with him, for having witnessed my mother celebrate nine decades on earth, for having shared so much *life* with both of them. The good fortune I had been envying in others was something I possessed, as well. It had simply been hidden beneath the thick shroud of my grief.

There was a time when my social media feed was just as active as the feeds of my friends and family. I would post nonstop about my adventures with my husband, about happy days spent hanging out with my mother, and about the joys of my world in general. Those memories are still mine, and they will never go away. I am less of a prolific poster nowadays, though, and I think it's because I'm spending more of my time really *living* rather than putting my life on display.

My reality has shifted, and it will continue to shift — as will yours. Like me, you may feel the greedy claws of jealousy grab hold of you as you move through the emotions surrounding your loss or losses. Know that this is okay and even natural, especially in this increasingly virtual culture of ours. It's hard, after all, to escape the picture-perfect perspectives that are forever coming at us through our phones and computers, and harder still to avoid comparing our seemingly sadder, emptier, less fulfilling lives to those that we see on our screens. Hard, but not impossible.

Though I don't believe that any emotion is ever wasted, I quickly found that I had no use for anger, resentment, and jealousy. Feeling those things was an important part of my journey, and it may be an important part of yours, too. I hope, however, that you will eventually choose to uncover your gratitude for the relationships you had with your lost loved ones, for the memories you made with them, and for the people who are around to support and care for you now.

Your thankfulness for what *was* — your rich history with whomever you lost — might be hiding in a box of old photos, a stash of past birthday cards, or a silly little anniversary gift. Your appreciation for what *is* might emerge from a bouquet of flowers left on your desk by a coworker, from a family member's standing invitation to Friday dinner, or from a friend's "just thinking of you" text or phone call. As you heal, things that seemed normal or insignificant or that were simply invisible prior to your loss have the potential to take on new value; to help you see how full your life has always been and how rich it will continue to be.

You have the power to rearrange your emotional outlook and to make decisions about how you want to feel. Jealous or grateful. Bitter or hopeful. This is one of the greatest gifts we humans have — and we have the ability to give it to ourselves whenever we choose.

GUILT AND REGRET

While we're exploring all these not so pleasant sensations, I'd be remiss if I didn't bring up guilt and regret — another powerful pair that can linger in our subconscious as we navigate our way through loss, hampering our ability to feel and even to desire joy.

Maybe I could have — should have — done more. I shouldn't have been so upset and yelled about something that now seems totally trivial. Why am I still here while they are gone? I don't deserve life any more than they did.

This is the type of mental chatter that ran on loop in the early stages of my grief. We humans like to control things, and when we can't... well, we'll try to do it, anyway. For a time, I wanted to turn back the clock and find those moments when I could have made a difference in my mother's or my husband's fate. Where my mother was concerned, should I have tried harder to convince her to accept treatment for her illness? Did she secretly want me to? Could I have done something more special to mark her last days of life? Could I have made her more comfortable as she slipped away? Had I been the best daughter I could be?

As to my husband, shouldn't I have seen that heart attack coming? There had to have been signs. How could I have missed them? Should I have paid more attention to his diet? Should I have asked him how he was feeling more often? And what about all the things on our shared bucket list that would now remain forever unfinished? Wasn't I the planner? Wasn't I the one who was supposed to have made sure we were on track to achieving all our dreams? Hadn't I failed us?

In a way, feeling guilty was something of a relief from the how-could-you-do-this-to-me, now-I'm-all-alone-and-it's-your-fault resentment I had previously directed toward the woman who had raised me and the man who had been my rock for forty years. Somehow, blaming myself felt less ugly than blaming the defenseless departed — and if I *really* wanted to pile on myself, I could shame myself for my outward resentment. The potential for self-sabotage is, you see, infinite.

But *did* I want to do that? When I stepped back to look at the mental gymnastics I was attempting in an effort to grasp the ever-elusive "Why?" behind death, I had to acknowledge that guilt and regret weren't providing any answers. They were just making me feel lousy. They were just two more emotions that I needed to recognize and release.

My mother, having enjoyed a vibrant, fulfilling life, and having loved and been loved beyond measure, had chosen to forgo treatment for her kidney problems. She was simply done, and she wanted to take her leave on her own terms. If I had decided that I wasn't going to blame her for that, what sense was there in blaming myself? And to question the care I had given her during our final week together — would I do that to someone else who had been in a similar position? Absolutely not.

In extreme, emotion-laden circumstances, we all muddle through the best we can, and at heart, I knew that I had done everything in my power to give my mom the best last week possible. On top of that, I had been allotted ample time to process her decision in her presence, to pre-grieve with her, and to share an extended goodbye. I had been fortunate. *We* had been fortunate. It just took me a minute to see that.

In my husband's case, choice hadn't been part of the equation. Had Will been given the chance to reflect on his heart attack, I imagine he would have been just as stunned as I was, and he definitely wouldn't have sent me on a guilt trip for having neglected to anticipate or prevent it. He had no clue that something was wrong, so how could I have known any better? If anything, he would have put an arm around me and said, "Jeanne, if I could've stuck around for another few years — or decades — with you, I would have. But all things considered, we had a pretty good run, didn't we?" He would not have wanted me to regret our "unfinished business" any more than he would have wanted me to feel responsible for his early exit. And he would have thought it preposterous that my life should come to a complete halt just because his had. Such a logical man.

Death is a fact of life. Guilt and regret don't have to be. If you are wrestling with these emotions as you grieve, I urge you to put them on trial. Do they have any basis in fact? When you review all the evidence surrounding your loss, can you really be found guilty of anything? Are you burying the many joyous memories and experiences you shared with your loved one under the infinite mountain of things that you *didn't* have a chance to accomplish because you truly think that, given more time, you could have scaled that impossible peak? Or are you using guilt and regret as shields so that you won't have to progress into a phase of acceptance?

I certainly was. Once I stopped the self-blame game, though, acceptance didn't seem nearly so scary. I chose to let guilt and regret go so that I could make peace with the passings of my mother and husband, and so that I could move forward with my life as they would have wanted me to do. I believe that you can do the same — and that whomever you lost would be happy to see you do it.

FAMILY

It's strange to think about what those who have passed away might want for us. When they were living, we would have just known. But with the loss of a person comes the loss of a relationship, and we survivors are left with a hole where that person's emotional and physical presence used to be.

So, how do we fill that hole? And how does if affect our relationships with our living family, friends, colleagues, and acquaintances? Figuring these things out, I discovered, is part of the business of grieving — one that I didn't quite grasp when my emotions were still as raw from my losses as my eyes were from crying.

There are many layers to the topic of relationships, so I'll take it piece by piece, starting close to home. Starting with family.

My mother was a true matriarch. A soft-spoken but strong Italian woman, she was the glue that held all the various parts of the extended family together. Everyone knew and loved "Aunt Jennie." She counseled, she comforted, she told the truth. She was steady as a rock, and no matter where a particular family member was, she was always within their reach when they needed her.

At the time she chose to leave this good earth, my mother was well on in her years, so though no one had been anticipating her death, it couldn't have been called an unusual occurrence. As such, many of the connections that had seemed so sturdy and constant when she was alive began to melt away rather rapidly. The glue was gone, and with it went the more distant relatives, who naturally, understandably drifted back to their lives.

I say "naturally" and "understandably" now, but at the time, I didn't see it that way. My mom was dead. How could all these people who once seemed to adore her as much as I did just... go on? Had they even taken time to acknowledge everything that she had done for us as a family — that she had done for *them* as individuals? Initially, my internal response to this apparent desertion was so intense that I felt physically hurt by it.

It's hard to recall exactly what I expected others to do. Maybe I was looking for a billboard that declared their affection in bold, illuminated letters: "WE LOVE YOU, AUNT JENNIE! YOU ARE MISSED!" Maybe I thought that their relationships with my mother would automatically be passed down to me; that those age-old connections she had nurtured would keep right on existing as they had for my entire life up to that point, but with me on the other end instead of her.

This was one of my first encounters with the idea that there are degrees to emotions. Today, it makes perfect sense to me that my love for my mother and my sorrow at her loss should have been far more intense than those same feelings within a second cousin or an in-law of an in-law. Of course these people adored and missed her. Of course they were sad that she was gone. But did I really imagine that their ties to her could be anywhere near as deep as mine was? Though it took me a while to come to this realization, I was able to view their behavior with more reason and compassion once I did.

The fallout from my husband's passing was more of an emotional rollercoaster, in part because it was so unexpected. In the days directly following Will's death, the immediate family — my two sons, their wives, and my young granddaughters — came together, and we all worked through the initial shock as a unit. The fact that it happened just before Christmas, when everyone's schedule was about to be placed on pause, anyway, bought us a little more time in each other's company.

But shortly after the holidays, my sons and their wives and children all had to get back to their lives. At first, they checked in regularly. Gradually, however, the calls became less frequent, and I started to feel that I alone was left mourning the loss. What I did not see then was just how much they were still struggling, as well. I *couldn't* see it, in fact, because of the physical distance between us, one son living an hour away and the other seven hours away.

In my blindness, I yearned for someone to feel exactly what I was feeling while simultaneously providing me with a dependable emotional anchor — never mind the contradictory nature of those two tasks. I certainly couldn't have served as another person's anchor at that time. I was a mess! But nonetheless, I desired and even expected those things of my children, the volatility of my internal environment hampering my ability to reason out the unique difficulties that *they* were facing. It was like I wanted them to pay me back for the many years I had spent caring for them; wanted them to bandage up my wounds and tell me everything would be okay; wanted them to fix the situation and to fix me.

Eventually, my vision cleared and I was able to acknowledge that my healing was not up to them. No one could make me happy again or erase my sorrow. I conceded that my feelings were and always would be my responsibility. I knew that I had to choose to feel something other than whatever it was that kept dragging me down.

The interesting thing is that I had never been one to pity myself, to play the victim, or to presume that other people could and should swoop in to save me from anything, including my own emotional prison. That behavior materialized in me as a result of a grief deeper than any that I had ever experienced, and the moment I saw it for what it was, I set about trying to correct it — because the last thing I wanted to do was to make other people feel bad on account of my suffering or feel guilty that they couldn't "cure" me.

Instead, I turned inward to seek the seeds of strength, resilience, and faith that had been brushed aside by pain, disorientation, and despair. And I found them. They had always been within me, but I had never noticed them because I hadn't needed to do so. Prior to my losses, I had simply *been* strong, resilient, and full of faith in myself and in my higher power. From that point on, however, I realized that I would have to *choose* to be those things. Once I came to that conclusion, I was able to open my heart and my mind to what my sons were going through — and to the fact that grief was operating very differently within each of us.

In terms of timing, my older son worked his way through grief on a path somewhat parallel to my own. When we had each made it to our separate places of understanding within, we were able to support each other reciprocally, as mother and son, rather than weighing one another down with volatile, unresolved emotions. I no longer had the urge to hold on for dear life, as a victim might, and he had wrapped his mind around the absence of the most important male figure in his world. We gave each other the opportunity to see beyond our shared loss, grounding ourselves in the relationship that had always existed between us — a bond that would never be the same without the presence of his father, my husband, but that had proven its resilience and significance through the trauma of death.

I must acknowledge the essential role my older son's wife played, as well, for as female spouses, we have a perspective in common. It was so valuable and validating for me to see a bit of myself reflected in her, and since that time, our relationship has only grown stronger and more dynamic. It is a gift to be able to support her in the experience of motherhood as she supported me in my many hours of need.

As to my younger son... His reaction to Will's passing took me a little longer to comprehend. He chose to distance himself from me and the rest of the family — from anything or anyone that would allow him to hear, see, or think about the emotions he wasn't yet ready to feel. We were part of a reality that he was unwilling or unable to face.

This behavior had me asking myself, "What did I do? Where did I go wrong? How can I help?" But I hadn't done anything, wrong or right, to prompt his actions, and I couldn't offer him a helping hand until he was prepared to receive it. He was choosing not to engage with me and the rest of the family because to do so would have meant unlocking the floodgates that he had constructed around his emotions. I had to release judgement, release my own need to help him as his mother, and give him room to grieve on his own time and terms.

So, family: It's complicated, and it becomes even more so in the wake of loss. As you grieve, keep that simple fact in mind. Notice how the emotions of everyone around you, even your closest relatives, are different from yours, and be careful not to criticize them or yourself for those differences. Censure is an additional weight that you do not need to bear. Also be aware of how the intensity and turbulence of your feelings may be effecting your perception and your ability to reason, and give yourself the space and grace to heal through them. Grieving takes time and an open mind, and try as we might, we will find no success in rushing or forcing the process for ourselves or for others.

FRIENDS

If reactions to loss within a family are wide ranging, they tend to be even more so in the relationship circles beyond. Tentative acquaintances can turn into close confidants; previously unknown friends of friends can become bosom buddies; the dearest of companions can drift out of touch. I experienced all of these things, to the extent that my current sphere of connections has a totally different look than it did prior to my losses, and prior to the loss of my husband, in particular.

In general, I felt that people began to view me "minus two" differently. Whether this was because my way of interacting with them had changed or because they were afraid of saying the wrong thing or because they saw grief as some sort of contagion, I couldn't have told you at the time. For quite a while, I was too much in the middle of my pain and sorrow to be fully aware of how my behavior toward others might have shifted, and I was definitely too internally tangled up to properly interpret their feelings toward me and my situation. In retrospect, I can see that there were adjustments being made on both sides of every relationship.

There were many people who couldn't do enough to comfort me or to help me "overcome my grief" — some only for the first week or two, others for a longer period. They meant well. But I found that even those who had lost loved ones of their own seemed to have forgotten that grief isn't about "overcoming" anything. It's about navigating through the feelings that death triggers, which is a journey that has to happen within.

Nonetheless, "call me anytime" and "I'm here whenever you need me" were frequent refrains for these folks, as was my personal favorite, "How are you *really* doing?" Even in my darkest moments, this question always gave me a bit of a laugh. I wondered if those who asked it were really ready to hear the truth, or if it would cause them to pass out from shock — because the truth was pretty gritty. My emotions were so all over the place that I couldn't keep track of my mental status from one moment to the next; I was sleeping far less than was necessary for a normal human body; I sometimes wondered if I knew the person I saw in the mirror each morning, and if whomever she was would actually make it through the day. Somehow, though, I was able to keep my head just clear enough to see the humor in overly innocent, well-intentioned questions, and this provided an occasional ray of relief.

Another subset of people seemed to have a hard time being around me, likely because they hadn't gone through any great loss and so had no way of empathizing. They didn't get that "making it better" wasn't really possible, and that their inability to "fix" me was not a personal failing. They couldn't comprehend the true value of a hug or a sympathetic word or a shoulder to cry on. They didn't know that all they needed to be was *there*. I don't blame them. With an event as drastic as the death of a loved one, it's nearly impossible to understand the emotional repercussions without having been on the front lines.

Ultimately, I found that most of my relationships came down to that magical gift and burden of choice — my own and that of those around me. While family ties will certainly shift following a loss, they are less apt to totally break than those we have with friends and acquaintances. It is common for people to drift in and out of our lives, but never more notably, I think, than in the shadow of grief.

The phrase "let's keep in touch" became a sort of red flag for me — an indicator that a relationship was about to end. Whether it was I or the people on the other side of these bonds who let them fade away usually wasn't apparent. Probably a bit of both. Perhaps they weren't prepared for the level of emotional involvement I was seeking at the height of my pain. Perhaps I knew in my gut that they couldn't provide the support I needed.

One thing is for sure: When it comes to what I look for in a relationship now, my priorities have shifted. While Will was around, I had more of a flexible policy with regards to maintaining old connections and forging new ones. Since most of my emotional needs were met at home, in my healthy, happy marriage, I had no reason to seek that kind of fulfillment from other sources. I don't think I even noticed how close or casual certain relationships were because I could just enjoy their unique energy without expecting anything more of them. After my husband's death, however, the deep well of love and soulful understanding that he and I had shared suddenly dried up, and I was confronted with a decision: I could either leave the well empty and live out the rest of my days as a hollow shell, or I could find a new form of meaning with which to fill it. I went the latter route.

As I dogpaddled through my grief, I began to experience quiet moments of choosing whether or not to keep up certain connections. I became hyperaware of the fact that some people were more willing and better able than others to stick with me through the ups and downs of emotional healing. These were the friends who knew how to embrace rather than to retreat from my intense, frequently volatile feelings; who both lent me their strength and fostered my own; who allowed me the space and the time to rebuild my inner world; who are still near and dear to me today. I have learned to cherish these bonds, and not to take them for granted as I may once have done.

In a way, my circle of friends and acquaintances has grown smaller because there are fewer people in it. But what it has lost in physical size, it has gained, with interest, in spiritual value and richness. This is not to say that I haven't formed any new relationships over the past few years. I've simply been more selective and thoughtful in doing so.

The fact is that the person I was before my life came crashing down is not the person who emerged from the rubble. I like to think that my essence is the same; that my sense of humor and my good will and my capacity to love, for instance, have not escaped me; that my best parts have evolved with me and actually become stronger as a result of the challenges I have faced. The way I look at the world, however, and the way I have chosen to exist within it are definitely different — and my relationship habits have had to catch up to that reality.

If you have yet to notice shifts in your post-loss relationships, I guarantee that you eventually will. Certain friendships or even close familial bonds may no longer feel as relevant, as fulfilling, or as healthy as they once did. In those cases, don't be afraid to reevaluate the space that they are taking up in your social sphere, because that space is invaluable. While *you* will survive through loss and grief — trust me: you will — not every relationship will survive with you. This type of change is natural and, I believe, necessary to the process of healing. Rather than fearing or avoiding these shifts, I hope that you will learn to welcome them and to view them as opportunities for growth — opportunities to make choices, to shape your new reality, and to fill that reality with people who will not only help you to feel again, but who will help you to feel *good*.

OVERDEPENDENCE AND INDEPENDENCE

There's one more type of relationship to address, and that's our relationship with relationships themselves. I know: What? Allow me to explain.

The moment we step out of that initial numbness phase that follows a personal loss — the moment emotions start to flood back into our inevitably underprepared systems — our survival instinct prompts us to seek handholds and footholds within our environment. Our minds, spirits, and even our bodies need tethering, and initially, tethers can be pretty easy to find.

If our loss impacted others in a similarly significant way, we will, for a time, have companions in our grief. This is what I experienced with my children immediately after losing Will. We were all distraught and off balance, and for the first few weeks, we were able to anchor one another.

Just beyond that inner circle of shared grief, we will find those who either knew the departed, who know us, or both. As I mentioned, some of these people will seem ready to give an arm, a leg, or any number of other invaluable possessions to help us through our pain.

In essence, there's nothing wrong with these cords of support. If we use them only enough to keep our heads above water until we're able to swim through grief and the emotions that come with it on our own, they can actually give the healing process a healthy forward push. It's when we begin to cling to the cords that they become counterproductive — and potentially harmful. This is very nearly what happened for me.

I spoke about the irrational expectations I held for my sons once we made it through the dicey early days following their father's death, when they returned to their homes and their work and their lives. That was my first taste of overdependence, and I'm grateful that I was able to identify and adjust my skewed perspective before it took its toll on our mother-child bonds.

But that revelation didn't stop me from falling into a comparable trap with that other group of commiserators — those outside my closest family who were invariably ready and willing to be of service. At first, I didn't even have to ask for anything. They were just there, whether I felt that I needed them or not. Eventually, however, I got used to their presence and their perpetual offers of support, so much so that I began to expect those things. And then I began to rely upon them.

When we're at our most vulnerable, we can get into the habit of allowing others to think for us, to choose for us, to protect us from the difficulty of having to "do" for ourselves. Without realizing it, we can mentally transfer responsibility for our wellbeing onto others, looking to them to solve our problems, to fill our most hollow hours, and to prevent us from sinking into states of anxiety, depression, or pain.

In my case, I wound up unconsciously — almost robotically — counting on close friends and relatives to create my life for me, silently asking them to forfeit their personal time in order to fill up mine. How unfair is that? Granted, relationships are a two-way street. These people were all intelligent adults capable of arriving at their own decisions and managing their own internal resources. I'm sure I didn't make it easy for them, though. It was probably obvious that I didn't know what I needed, and whether they knew or not, they could at least satisfy themselves with having tried to help someone they loved.

It took me a while to notice how I was behaving, but when the realization came, it was swift. For quite some time after Will's death, I had a standing dinner date with a few relatives. The whole setup was like clockwork. Every week, on the same day and at the same hour, they would drive to my house, pick me up, and whisk me away to a restaurant of their choosing. There was no effort involved on my part. I was just taken along for the ride.

Perhaps all that sounds normal enough. But our unspoken follow-the-leader arrangement would continue once we were inside the selected restaurant, with me seated in a chair and at a table that I'm sure I had no part in choosing. I finally caught on to what was happening one evening when we were looking over a menu, and I was told, "You always get this entrée when we come here." Something suddenly clicked in my head. Did I really "always" have the same dish at that restaurant? If so, was I the one who had originally chosen it? Did I actually want it this time? Had I ever wanted it?

Many ideas fell into place at that moment. Clearly, "Jeanne the widow" — a role played with uncanny accuracy by me — had once been so all over the place emotionally that I hadn't seemed capable of ordering a meal, much less of deciding what restaurants I liked or when I felt like dining out. It's amazing how such basic acts can be made so insurmountable by grief.

After that incident, I committed to making a conscious effort to do small things on my own, without any external input and without throwing in the towel when a challenge arose. I chose to become my own responsibility — more so than I ever had been, I think — and to allow others simply to be in my life rather than to try to run it for me. What, when, and where I wanted to eat comprised one small collection of choices on a growing list that, when taken as a whole, formed a telling picture of how I wanted to exist.

I had never been a computer whiz, but if I had to make up my mind about something I didn't understand, I turned to Google, teaching myself whatever it was I needed to know. If I needed expert advice, I figured out who the experts were and asked them annoying questions. Of course, all this cost me more time, energy, and courage than it would have to call a friend or relative who could have "fixed" things in a flash. But by then, I was ready. Scary and frustrating as it was to take ownership of my life, it gradually became easier, and all the while, I kept reminding myself that support would be there for me whenever I asked for it — or rather, whenever I *chose* to ask for it.

We all need help to fumble our way through grief, especially in the early stages, when we are still too emotional to make even the most fundamental decisions, much less those that might be beneficial to us. In emerging from the immediate darkness of loss, however, it is critical to adjust how heavily we lean on these external resources; to slowly shift the balance of responsibility from others to ourselves; to do the deep work of redefining and reestablishing our independence.

The timeline for this process, like that for grief on the whole, is different for everyone. I can't tell you exactly how long it took me to feel fully independent again, and if I could, I don't think that I would. Your experience will be unique, and developing a sensitivity to your emotional and logistical needs will be part of it.

You may, for instance, find speaking with a therapist or joining a grief support group to be valuable as you attempt to moderate your emotional reliance on family and friends. Objective input from those who fully grasp what you are going through, either firsthand or via professional training, may prevent you from backsliding into old habits by providing you with a broader perspective on healing and by reminding you that you are not actually broken — that you do not need to be fixed.

I was fortunate enough to discover that an acquaintance of mine was navigating the murky waters of grief at the same time I was, and we both found solace and fortification in each other's company over the course of many late-night phone calls. Though our losses were different, we were facing similar internal struggles, which meant that our connection was balanced, with neither of us at risk of becoming overly needy. We understood one another. That was enough.

My general guidance on the topic of dependence and its various degrees is simply to pay attention to who is making your choices, large and small — not so that you can judge yourself for the level of assistance you require at any given moment, but so that you can slowly begin to take your choices back, one at a time, when you're ready. And if you're listening to your gut, you will know when you're ready.

LONELINESS AND BEING ALONE

Regaining independence is a major achievement, and for the most part, it feels pretty great. Funny thing about being independent, though: It can often mean spending quite a bit of time alone.

This is not necessarily a bad thing. In fact, alone time can actually help you to get to know yourself — which, as I've mentioned, is an important step in healing through loss. It's loneliness that you have to be careful of, because that can set you back.

Loneliness and being alone... Yes, they are two different things! Somehow, even amidst my grief, I recognized the distinction fairly quickly. I saw that being on my own was just a fact I had to deal with. It was concrete — a physical status that I could change by choosing a different environment.

Loneliness, on the other hand, is not something that can be outwardly seen or manually shifted, though it is certainly felt within the body. I first noticed it as a heavy sadness centered in my heart. The sensation was of having lost a vital part of myself that could not be replaced — yet the knowledge that the missing part was really gone for good hadn't quite settled in yet. The kinetic energy of my love was searching for its most loyal match, but that match was no longer available. That was loneliness. Sometimes it would creep into my chest with a quiet, persistent frenzy; sometimes it would wake me up with loud howls of frustration and despair. It could appear while I was in my house with only my cat for company or in the middle of a room filled with people. Even after my grief peaked, loneliness was as unpredictable as it was all-encompassing.

On a basic level, loneliness was simply the absence of companionship with my husband. At the time he passed away, we had long been empty nesters, and we'd gotten into the habit of taking at least one adventure each weekend. If football wasn't on, we could be found road-tripping to a vineyard for lunch, testing out a new local movie theater, or even just scrounging around the nearest big-box store for the best deals of the day. We weren't scaling Mount Everest or anything, but whatever we decided to do, we were in it together. From planning to execution, the intimacy of our connection was a huge part of the experience.

Once Will was out of the picture, the notion of adventuring in and of itself seemed empty and unfulfilling. I was more alone than I had been in forty years. Actually, because I had gotten married so young, I was more alone than I had been in my entire sixty-two years. That was a given.

What was *not* a given, as it turned out, was that I should constantly feel lonely within my solo status. I discovered that I could choose to let the emotional void within me remain open, allowing it to drag my energy down and sap my spirit dry, or I could make up my mind to fill it with fresh sensations and ideas, giving myself the chance to feel whole again — not in the same way that I had when my husband was with me, but to a similar extent. This took some adjusting, both in how I thought and how I acted.

For me, the biggest shock in being alone — the first hurdle I had to clear — was the silence. After the initial mourning period, when my relatives had returned to their own lives and the visits from dear friends became less frequent, I had the TV on constantly. It didn't ask me how I was doing or offer to make me tea or gently point out that my socks were mismatched, but it was reliable company, nonetheless. Even once I was able to turn it off, I stayed on my own at home for quite some time, feeling lonely and allowing that loneliness to run my state of mind. But I knew things couldn't remain that way for the rest of my days. Quietly supportive as my cat was, he couldn't replace people. I needed human interaction — and it wasn't going to magically come to me.

Treating myself to a nice meal in my own kitchen was a good starting point because it was an experience that I could translate directly into the outside world. I just had to take the whole scenario and move it to a different setting, which is how I ended up in that cafe with the cup of coffee and the muffin that I enjoyed so much. I had been alone and I had still, at that point, been feeling lonely. But I had made a move in the right direction.

The next step was to pop my head out of my silent, protective shell by speaking with the people around me when I went out. This is what I did during my first solo trip to the big-box store, pushing myself to talk to anyone within a few feet of me. In the clothing section, I struck up a conversation about proper cashmere sweater care with a woman I didn't know from Eve. Amongst the kitchenware, I explored the benefits of wooden over silver spoons with another complete stranger. Did any of these brief connections, these surface exchanges, hold a candle to what I once had with Will? Definitely not. But they did reignite some small specks of light inside of me, and that was enough to keep me going — to keep me from sliding back into the invisible depths of loneliness.

As time went on, deciding whether to eat out or in, whether to curl up on the couch with a book or to go shopping, became less challenging. The realization that I could feel equally lonely in any of those contexts was liberating because it showed me that I could flip my feelings whenever I needed to do so. If I woke up with a sense of anxious isolation, I could turn breakfast into a social experience either by calling a friend, or by heading to a diner to be around other people while I ate and to chat with my server for a spirit boost. If I felt the need to make a few temporary friends, I could head to a craft store — which, by the way, is *the best* place to find sociable people because they're usually eager to chat about their latest projects. I've learned a lot at craft stores.

Being alone and being lonely are matters of choice. We can choose to be one or the other, both or neither. To some degree, loneliness is still active within me. I believe that it will never truly go away. It will show up every once in a while to remind me of a different time, a different life, and at those moments, I will feel my heartstrings stretching again, tears welling up, sadness setting in... But I will never allow loneliness to rule me as it once did. I've gotten better at understanding it, at accepting it, at riding its unpredictable waves rather than suppressing them — because, as with every other emotion that grief revealed to me, I found that suppression was not a great way to combat loneliness. Trying to lock a feeling up and hide the key just leaves me numb again, and numbness is, as we've already established, no way to live. It was only by letting my loneliness out that I learned to view it as an occasional companion rather than an unbearable burden, and to recognize it as something separate from being alone.

This is no easy mental move to make. It takes time, courage, and patience. It also takes a willingness not to let your memories of what was — beautiful though they may be — limit what is and what could be. I've said it before and I'll say it again: Your memories aren't going anywhere. They belong to you, and they won't disappear just because the person associated with them is no longer around. If you try to hold on to them too tightly, though, they can pull you backward, leaving you alone *and* feeling lonely.

So, how do you move forward on your own without pushing the past away or blocking opportunities to create your best possible present and future? My basic guidance is to start small. First, just notice when and where loneliness is poking holes in your heart and soul. This will probably be painful, and it's okay to sit with that pain for a while. But don't stay there for long. Once you've determined where those holes are, look for ways to fill them with specks of light from the world around you — anything that makes you feel alive, if only for a few moments. Maybe chatting up people at a discount store or hearing your barista's backstory is not your thing. But maybe asking a friend if they're available for lunch or a movie date is. Whatever tiny steps you choose to make, the goal remains the same: to restore, and maybe even to improve, the internal balance that the loss of a loved one upsets so that, in time, you can become your own closest companion.

At the end of the day, we are all alone, no matter who is or is not by our side. If you make an effort to fill yourself up with new interests and adventures and passions, however, the idea of being alone will no longer hollow you out. It will set you free.

CREATIVITY

While I was figuring out how to be alone without being lonely — and really, how to feel all my feelings without allowing them to engulf me — I rediscovered an internal asset that I had long taken for granted: creativity.

I've never considered myself an artist. I have no formal artistic training to speak of. But I can see now that my lengthy career as a hairdresser offered a subtle outlet for my creative mind, and that the satisfaction I took from my job must have come, in part, from the artistry it allowed me to explore.

So I guess it was only natural that in the midst of my journey through grief, creativity came calling at just the right moment. It started with something I saw on TV: an artist crafting a beautiful flower out of clay. This image rustled up a memory from my childhood — a memory of my mother making little model greenhouses full of tiny flowers, and enlisting me and my siblings to help. Something in my heart sparked at this recollection, and instinctively, I seized it.

My mom, resourceful woman that she was, had used homemade bread dough as "clay." On the TV program I was watching, however, the artist was working with polymer clay, so the very next day, I went out and bought some — and then I started to play. I was hooked, instantly. The act of holding and molding clay gave me a physical focus beyond the sense of absence caused by my losses; gave my hands and arms something to do other than to feel empty; gave my mind a purpose other than to process pain. It also allowed me to remember my mother with happiness rather than with sorrow, and to feel gratitude for her life in a richer way.

Fueled by the fulfillment of this first foray into art making, I became curious about other mediums. I learned about resin, how versatile it is, and how much I could craft with it. I started to dabble with paint, teaching myself how to mix colors and discovering that ordinary objects could be used as "brushes." Essentially, I built up an arsenal of creative skills and supplies, and then I began to blend them together. Paint and resin, shells and stones, metal and wire, feathers and fabrics... I mixed and matched. I made mistakes and masterpieces and more things than I knew what to do with.

As I launched into each new project, my desire to create grew, and so did my excitement. This was a big deal because up to then, I think I had bottled up my ability to be excited; had forgotten what it was to desire something other than what I had lost and could never have back. Unconsciously, I may even have stopped believing that those sensations were possible for me. I didn't realize it at the time, but my capacity to create was bringing me back to life.

When we lose people whom we love so dearly that they have become a part of us, something within us dies along with them. That may sound horrible, but if you've been there, you know what I mean. Death is not just the end of a life; it is a part of life for those of us who have lost someone — and so is recognizing the beautiful things that can bloom from it.

Perhaps even more rewarding than the internal pleasure I experienced in sculpting and painting and crafting and creating in general was the response I received from those closest to me when I began to open up about my projects. Family members and friends expressed admiration and enthusiasm for what I was doing, and they encouraged me to keep at it. They also suggested that I share my art with a larger audience. Intimidating as this idea was, I took it to heart.

Finally, near the beginning of 2021 — almost two years after my mother had passed and just over one since my husband had followed her — I began to post photos of my creations to Instagram, including a little note of inspiration or hope or kindness with each one. It felt good. I was giving back to the world in a way I never would have known that I could had I not suffered and struggled and chosen to thrive through grief. I had found a reason to get up in the morning beyond just having breakfast. I had remembered what a gift it is both to feel joy and to spread it, as well.

While my art is no replacement for the relationships I had with my mother and husband, it has filled some portion of the vast chasm that my losses opened up. In times of trauma, creativity can act as a lifeline, tapping into a part of the brain where difficult emotions tend to get stuck, and then inviting those emotions out. I can't tell you how much of a relief it is to feel that psychological release. You will simply have to experience it for yourself.

If sculpting and painting don't appeal to you, search around for other creative outlets that might. I truly believe that there is something out there for everyone. If silly little poems pop into your head every other minute, grab a pen and put it to paper. Maybe you'll discover that your words are not so silly at all. If you love music, try picking up an instrument or even composing something. Maybe you're a virtuoso waiting to emerge. If you danced as a child and have always wanted to start again, find a local or virtual class to take. If you enjoy baking, buy yourself a new recipe book and hit the kitchen.

There is no noteworthy risk in testing any of these creative waters. The real risk lies in not testing them at all, for you are the only person capable of unleashing your innermost talents — and of allowing yourself to heal through their beauty.

SPIRITUALITY

One of the most rewarding aspects of creativity for me is how connected it makes me feel. In the most concrete sense, the artistic projects I chose while I was at the height of my grief were physically and mentally engaging, drawing my body and mind out of my pain and providing them with a new, tangible focus. But action was also happening on a higher level, both within and beyond my soul. I felt more tuned in to the universe — to something greater than myself.

In spite of my Catholic upbringing, I don't adhere to any specific religion. I am, however, a very spiritual person with a firm belief in a divine entity — in a God that exists for everyone who chooses to believe. Following Will's death, my despair had dragged me so far below the surface of life that I doubted my ability to dig myself back up again. But even then, I never gave up my faith. I did not feel that it had failed me or that it was trying to teach me a lesson through trauma. On the contrary, my vision of God has always been marked by unconditional love and support; by open grace and guidance, in good times and in bad. My higher power has had my back since the day I was born, and that fact remained true throughout my grieving process.

I will never say that my losses were gifts. That's going too far. But to my *own* dying day, I will be grateful for the opportunity that loss granted me to strengthen my bond with God and to grow spiritually. Amidst all of my emotional turmoil — the sadness, the fear, the anger and resentment, the jealousy, the guilt and regret, the loneliness — I could have let my faith falter, fracture, or fully disintegrate. I could have questioned my higher power, accused it of having betrayed me, or blamed it for having neglected to take care of two souls that I loved more dearly than my own. I'm aware that many people do this, and I cannot judge them for it. But that was not my path.

Something deep within me — some profound, unwavering sense of "knowing" — told me to hold on to my belief system at all costs. Abandoning it wasn't even an option. My spiritual practices had always given me strength, and I was confident that they would continue to do so even as my world was collapsing around me. I was not wrong.

Loss will change you. Grieving will change you. These changes may challenge your belief system, and that's okay. But without telling you what that belief system should look like (because that's up to you), I'll say that I don't recommend obliterating it altogether. As with every aspect of life after loss, if the "old way" doesn't feel right anymore, you might need to make conscious adjustments, reevaluating how you practice your faith and even who or what is on the other end of it. Meditation may prove a useful tool on this front as it can create a safe time and space for you to turn within and identify your unique needs. Don't be afraid to try new things and to believe in a different way.

Wherever your spiritual journey takes you, trust that you are not alone on it — that a universal energy greater than any one of us exists at all times. We need only open our hearts and minds in order to receive its support.

SIMPLE GIFTS

Over the course of the past three years, life has dealt me some great challenges. My intention in sharing my journey was to bring a perspective to the experience of loss and grief that I hadn't found anywhere when I could have used it most. Understanding how loss can completely dismantle the structure of one's world, how grief and the emotions associated with it can disable one's basic thinking skills, how overwhelming it can be to define one's identity when it is so completely intertwined with that of someone who is no longer around — this all happened in real time for me, and I felt more than a little lost within the experience. I was just not prepared.

Maybe there *is* no way to prepare for the impact of a deep personal loss. Yet if my story provides any solace to others who are struggling, then it has been well worth the writing. It has, I feel, been an extraordinary series of gifts. Again, I don't mean that the losses themselves were gifts, but much of what came with them… Let me explain.

Loss, I now see, is the complete absence of something one once had, and the subsequent departure of what one was when that "something" still existed. As a concept, it is ultimately much simpler to grasp than grief. Grief is an endless, multifaceted, soul-piercing energy that one copes with every day — learning how to manage it and to move with and through it. Both loss and grief are still present within me, but they have become less crushing with time, and they have taught me an indispensable lesson: how to live with more simplicity and yet more meaning. This, to me, is a gift.

The process of reevaluating relationships has been another challenge with unexpected rewards. Giving up the feeling that I needed to be everything to everyone was a difficult but game-changing achievement. It enabled me to let go of relationships that I had never realized were one-sided, and to build stronger, healthier, more fulfilling connections with those who truly care. This is a gift.

Discovering that I could enjoy my own company, that I could be alone without being lonely, was also revolutionary. Now, rather than worrying about whether or not I can even make it through a few solitary hours, I regularly find myself deciding which book I want to read, which movie I want to watch, or what I want to cook for dinner on a solo evening in. I have more choices because I have less fear of me, myself, and I. This is a gift.

And art... Though I stumbled into it relatively late in life, I can no longer imagine my world without it! Being an artist has shown me what it means to keep trying in the face of failure — and that supposed failures can often result in the most beautiful creations. It has shown me that there are infinite possibilities for me to explore as long as I keep my soul open. This is a gift.

Feeling secure in myself and my surroundings, developing courage and a sense of adventure, understanding what it really means to *breathe* rather than allowing emotions to overwhelm me and inhibit my decision-making — these, too, are gifts that I have come to cherish.

But the greatest gift of all has been reality itself, because the reality in which I am currently living is something that I have designed; something that I have built, one choice at a time. I value my past and I have faith in my future. I also know that I cannot exist in either of those places. I can only be in this day, in this moment, embracing the choices I have made and the opportunities that have arisen from them.

On the second anniversary of Will's death, I received a beautiful flower arrangement from a friend who has helped me through some very tough times

— times when I was nearly swallowed by my emotions. The card that accompanied the arrangement carried a simple message that I feel came from the heart of the universe to help me and everyone now reading these words to face loss. To paraphrase, the message was this:

> Today is a fixed point in time. There is what came before and there is what will come after. If we stop to think about our lives as a continuous series of these fixed points, we can probably identify one or two moments of great change along the timeline. These are the moments that teach us to be *in* the moment, and that allow us to become more completely ourselves.

For me, this revelation occurred when — well after my mother and husband had left this world — I released my grip on the past and chose to move forward in a new way, not forgetting the existence I had once known, but not allowing it to hold me hostage, either.

The last three years have been marked by many such smaller moments as I continue to discover how I want my life to unfold. This is still a daily practice for me, and it is not always comfortable. But given the chance, I would not go back to my former mindset. Past, present, future — these concepts mean something different to me now. They are connected to one another in new ways, and I am connected to them in new ways, too. I now understand that my life is not shaped by time, but by the choices I make over the course of it.

It is my sincerest wish that my words will be your trusty companions, your perennial support system, as you move through the most challenging moments caused by your loss. Perhaps you are in one of those moments right now. If so, take this opportunity to simply breathe. Breathe in the life that is being created around you and breathe out the life that you are creating. Honor yourself — who you were, who you are, and who you still have yet to become — for no matter how lost you are *feeling* at any given time, you are not, in fact, lost. You are right here, right now. And this is just where you need to be.

DEDICATION

I dedicate this book to my husband. Will meant so much to so many people. His constant goal was to share every bit of wisdom he had with other people in order to lift them up and to show them the way to living a better life than they could imagine. He believed in the power of knowledge and in the duty of those who have it to offer it to others. He believed in everyone's right to learn. He believed that we are all capable of creating the reality in which we wish to exist if only we choose to do so.

This wisdom was Will's greatest gift to me — beyond his love, of course, which did not die with him, but remains alive and strong within me. If I have managed to convey either of these things by telling my story, then I feel that I have carried on where he left off when he departed this world.

I wrote a short poem shortly after he died, and I will share it here:

> If I had one more thing to tell you, what would it be?
> If I had one more day to travel with you, where would we go?
> Would saying that I love you have been enough?
> I don't know. I never got the chance to say those three simple words that express so much.

> I say them now: I love you.

> There was never enough time to do the things we planned to do.
> So I will learn to live the life that I was given with joy, gratitude, and respect for the being that I am.

Time seems to limit the ability in which we encase ourselves.
But there are no limits to time, only choices we make in the time that we have been given.

I love you!

Will always said, "We only have so many heartbeats, so let's use them to live life to its fullest." Trust me: He did.

(To my family that knew him so well, I am wearing the T-shirt!)

BIO

Jeanne Bundy was born, raised, and currently lives in New England. She is a retired hairstylist, hairdressing instructor, and salon manager, and she currently teaches a crafting class while developing her own artistry in a variety of mediums. She is also an intuitive specializing in oracle, tarot, and angel card readings. Through both her art and her spiritual practices, she seeks to inspire and encourage others to create the reality in which they wish to live.

As a Navy wife, Bundy traveled the world with her husband and their two sons before returning to the East Coast upon her husband's retirement. She is the proud grandmother of five grandchildren and the guardian of a devoted cat.

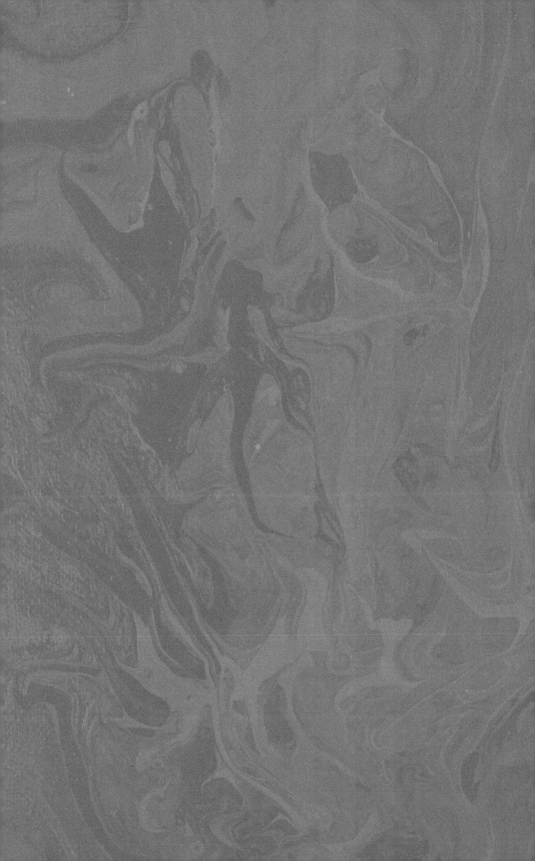

PORTFOLIO

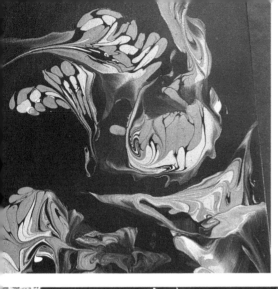

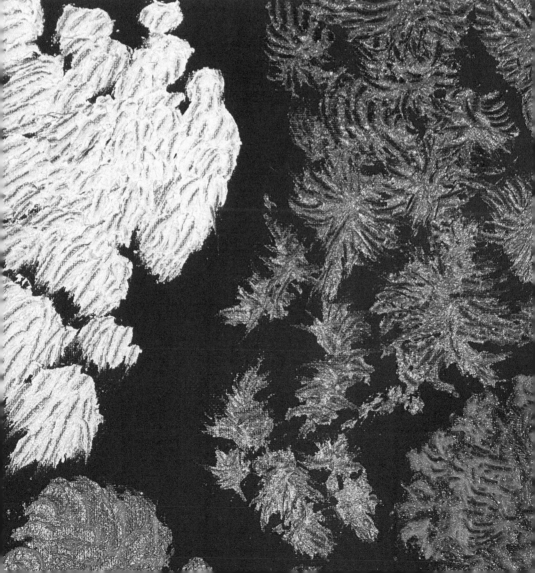

CPSIA information can be obtained
at www.ICGtesting.com
Printed in the USA
BVHW021658090722
641740BV00022B/182